# Good Governance in Egypt

## LEGISLATIVE DRAFTING MANUAL FOR BETTER POLICY

This work is published under the responsibility of the Secretary-General of the OECD. The opinions expressed and arguments employed herein do not necessarily reflect the official views of OECD member countries.

This document, as well as any data and any map included herein, are without prejudice to the status of or sovereignty over any territory, to the delimitation of international frontiers and boundaries and to the name of any territory, city or area.

**Please cite this publication as:**
OECD (2019), *Good Governance in Egypt: Legislative Drafting Manual for Better Policy*, OECD Publishing, Paris, *https://doi.org/10.1787/g2g9dd64-en*.

ISBN 978-92-64-31143-5 (print)
ISBN 978-92-64-31144-2 (pdf)

# *Foreword*

Laws and regulations have an impact on all aspects of everyday life. While good regulation contributes to well-functioning markets and societies, poor regulation may undermine them by imposing undue costs on businesses and citizens.

In the MENA region, good regulation is increasingly recognised as a precondition for strengthening the rule of law and building more resilient societies. The Arab Republic of Egypt has placed an emphasis on pursuing regulatory reform and prepared the first Egyptian legislative drafting guide to promote uniform quality in rulemaking.

This report sheds light on the role of legislative drafting guides in enhancing regulatory quality and good governance, and provides evidence from OECD and MENA countries on the preparation and implementation of the legislative drafting guides. In particular, the report assesses Egypt's legislative drafting guide in light of the 2016 OECD-MENA Regional Charter for Regulatory Quality, the 2012 OECD Recommendation of the Council on Regulatory Policy and Governance and international good practices. It then makes specific policy recommendations to guide the implementation of the Egyptian Legislative Drafting Manual.

This report builds on the OECD's expertise and policy knowledge acquired through dialogue among peer-countries in its Public Governance and Regulatory Policy Committees, its networks in the MENA-OECD Governance Programme, as well as the OECD instruments that codify good practices and standards in regulatory policy and public governance. In particular, the 2012 OECD Recommendation of the Council on Regulatory Policy and Governance sets out the principles of good regulatory governance and calls for open, transparent and inclusive processes in rulemaking to ensure that regulations serve the public interest.

The report is part of the MENA Transition Fund Project "The Rule of Law in Egypt" under the G7 Deauville Partnership, implemented in partnership with the Ministry of Justice of Egypt, the OECD and the African Development Bank. It is based on the findings of peer-to-peer exchanges, capacity-building activities, technical workshops and a series of study visits to OECD countries, including Canada, France, Italy, the Netherlands and Spain, which have been conducted since 2014. It is addressed to Egyptian officials in charge of legal drafting and regulatory policy. The OECD would like to thank the government officials and OECD peers for their commitment to the partnership, as well as the MENA Transition Fund of the G7 Deauville Partnership for their financial support.

# *Acknowledgements*

This report is published by the OECD Public Governance Directorate under the guidance of Marcos Bonturi, Director of Public Governance and the strategic direction of Martin Forst, Head of Governance Reviews and Partnerships Division.

Under the direct supervision of Miriam Allam, Head of the MENA-OECD Governance Programme, this report was authored by Gamze Igrioglu from the OECD Secretariat. The Report benefited from valuable comments from Nikolai Malyshev, Head of Regulatory Policy Division.

Particular thanks are expressed to Justice Hanni Hanna, Judge Magued Sobhi, Edward Donelan, Jean-Jacques Hible, Carina Sugden and William Robinson for their comments. Many thanks are also expressed to Filippo Cavassini, Eric Combes, Sherif Fawzi, Jean-Christophe Geiser, Sébastien Jeannard, Maggie Kamel, Mohamed Refai, Wolfgang Rusch, Wim Voermans and Helen Xanthaki for their contributions. Daisy Knox-Murphy provided logistical support, and Andrea Uhrhammer, Ciara Muller, Amelia Godber and Roxana Glavanov provided editing and publishing support.

The OECD would like to thank the government of the Arab Republic of Egypt, especially the Ministry of Justice and the Ministry of Investment and International Cooperation, for their active engagement, coordination and assistance in completing this report. The OECD would like to express particular thanks to H.E. Justice Mohamed Hosam Ahmed Ali Abdel-Reheem, Minister of Justice and H.E. Dr. Sahar Nasr, Minister of Investment and International Cooperation for their commitment to the partnership. The OECD would like to thank the African Development Bank for their cooperation.

The report is a contribution of the MENA-OECD Governance Programme within the scope of "Strengthening the Rule of Law: Effective and transparent delivery of justice and rule-making in Egypt" project, supported financially by the MENA Transition Fund Project of the G7 Deauville Partnership.

# *Table of Contents*


**Executive Summary** ........................................................................................................... 9

**Introduction** .................................................................................................................... 11

    References ..................................................................................................................... 13
    Notes ............................................................................................................................. 13

**Chapter 1. Implementing a better legislation policy** ................................................. 15

    Functions of legislation and importance of legislative quality ................................... 16
    Link between legislative and regulatory quality ......................................................... 19
    The role of legislative drafting manuals ..................................................................... 20
    Good practices ............................................................................................................. 21
    Characteristics of good legislative drafting manuals .................................................. 25
    References ..................................................................................................................... 29

**Chapter 2. The Egyptian Manual for Legislative Drafting** ..................................... 31

    Legislative Drafting Process in Egypt ........................................................................ 32
        Initiation and Drafting of Legislation ................................................................... 32
        Legislation proposed by the government ............................................................... 33
        Legislation proposed by the members of the parliament ....................................... 34
    Current Challenges ...................................................................................................... 36
    Egyptian Legislative Drafting Manual ....................................................................... 37

**Chapter 3. The Way Forward** .................................................................................... 41

    Implementation of the Egyptian Legislative Drafting Manual ................................... 42
    Specific Recommendations .......................................................................................... 42
    References ..................................................................................................................... 46


## Boxes


Box 1. The 2016 OECD-MENA Regional Charter for Regulatory Quality ......................... 12
Box 1.1. The 2012 OECD Recommendation of the Council on Regulatory Policy and Governance ... 17
Box 1.2. Legislative quality ............................................................................................... 18
Box 1.3. Germany ............................................................................................................... 21
Box 1.4. The Palestinian Authority .................................................................................... 22
Box 1.5. Switzerland ........................................................................................................... 23
Box 1.6. The Netherlands ................................................................................................... 24
Box 1.7. The European Union ............................................................................................. 25
Box 1.8. The United Kingdom ............................................................................................ 26
Box 1.9. France ................................................................................................................... 28

# *Executive Summary*

The 2012 OECD Recommendation of the Council on Regulatory Policy and Governance demonstrates that good regulatory management helps stimulate economic activity at both domestic and international levels. A well-functioning regulatory framework enables efficient markets and helps protect citizens against financial, economic and societal uncertainties. Law drafting techniques and procedures have a direct impact on the effectiveness of legislation and regulatory quality. Transparent and coherent legislative drafting procedures help promote public participation in the rule-making process, foster trust in the justice system, reinforce the rule of law and create an enabling business environment where citizens and businesses can identify their rights and obligations.

This report provides an understanding of how legislative drafting guides enhance legislative and regulatory quality. It provides evidence from the OECD and MENA countries on the preparation and implementation of legislative drafting guides and assesses the Egyptian Legislative Drafting Manual *vis-à-vis* OECD recommendations and international good practices. The report concludes with tailored policy recommendations for implementing the Egyptian Legislative Drafting Manual. In particular, it highlights the following key areas where further efforts could maximise the potential of the Egyptian Legislative Drafting Manual as a tool for obtaining better outcomes from legislation:

- **Ensure that the Manual is embedded into a broader "whole-of-government" policy for regulatory governance and supported by application of regulatory policy tools.** Consideration could be given to tools such as the of ex post and ex ante regulatory impact analysis (RIA), public consultations and stakeholder engagement, review of stock of legislation, administrative simplification, transparency and communication, alternatives to regulation; and ex post evaluation as a whole across the government.

- **Ensure high-level political commitment and sustained support for the effective implementation of the Manual. All parties engaged in legislative drafting should also commit to follow them.** Based on OECD experience, a formal announcement and commitment by the government calling for proper application of the legislative drafting instructions is critical for ensuring manuals can achieve their intended goals.

- **Design and publish a coherent and "whole-of-government" operational strategy for implementing the Egyptian Legislative Drafting Manual.** The strategy should cover the key steps in the implementation of the Manual while allocating clear responsibilities across relevant stakeholders and introducing timelines. The strategy should help legal drafters understand how applying the Manual can help improve the quality of legislation. It should also include a communications strategy to raise awareness and ensure sustained support for the implementation of the Manual. The strategy could introduce short- and medium-term goals to facilitate the monitoring of the progress.

- **Commit to reporting regularly on the implementation of the measures outlined in the operational strategy and the Legislative Drafting Manual.** The systemic application of monitoring and evaluation tools can help assess the effectiveness of implementation, reveal potential bottlenecks and encourage the formulation of appropriate responses.

- **Update and revise the Manual regularly, based on feedback provided by users on their experience of working with this tool on a daily basis.** The experience of OECD countries demonstrates that legislative drafting manuals need to adapt to the dynamic legal and regulatory environment as well as to the daily needs of legislative drafters.

- **Establish solid consultation and feedback mechanisms as well as an institutionalised working party tasked with updating the Manual.** Many OECD countries have introduced specific consultation and feedback mechanisms to help obtain constant feedback from manual users. Establishing a working party of relevant stakeholders can ensure the transparency of the process and enable collaboration across different institutions. Consultation methods need to be institutionalised for effective feedback, monitoring and evaluation. In addition, a network could be formed to help create buy-in to the Manual across different institutions and departments, and to keep the Manual up to date.

- **Pilot the Manual across different institutions and ministries; report user feedback to the working party to update and revise the Manual.** The Legislative Drafting Manual is the first of its kind in Egypt. Expecting immediate systemic application of the Manual across the government could be unrealistic given the uneven capacities and skills across public institutions. Piloting the Manual in different ministries and bodies could be a useful way to introduce the Manual, test its applicability; and reveal potential challenges.

- **Ensure that the Manual is publicly accessible and widely disseminated.** It is of vital importance that all parties engaged in law making have access to the Manual and could benefit from it. The Manual should be publicly available online as well as on the internal webpages of public institutions. Easy access to the Manual is crucial for raising awareness about its presence and to ensure its effective utilisation.

- **Introduce special software packages incorporating drafting guidance into the computer systems.** Drafting assistance tools have been introduced across a number of OECD countries to apply legislative drafting manuals more effectively and easily. These software packages also provide legal drafters with practical help that corresponds to their daily needs.

- **Provide trainings, seminars and workshops on legislative drafting principles, use of the Manual and legislative drafting software tools to all stakeholders engaged in legislative drafting**. It is essential to ensure that legislative drafters have adequate capacities and skills to benefit from the Manual and to produce quality legislation. Institutionalised legislative drafting training programmes in government, civil service training bodies or universities introducing legal drafters to the use of Manuals and legislative drafting software tools can contribute to raise awareness and build necessary skills among legal drafters.

# *Introduction*

This report is written for decision makers, policy makers, public officials and the international community working on better regulation and legislation. The report sheds light on the role of legislative drafting manuals in enhancing legislative and regulatory quality and promoting good governance; and provides evidence and good practices from the OECD countries in the preparation and implementation of the legislative drafting manuals. In particular, the report focuses on the first Egyptian legislative drafting manual[1], which is prepared by the Ministry of Justice of Egypt with the support of the OECD. This report aims to assess the legislative drafting manual of Egypt, which was launched in July 2018 by the Ministry of Justice of Egypt, in light of good practice as outlined in the 2016 Charter and 2012 Recommendation; and provide recommendations for making these legislative drafting instructions more operational and effective. The report is prepared as part of the MENA Transition Fund Project "The Rule of Law in Egypt" of the G7 Deauville Partnership, implemented in partnership with the Ministry of Justice and the African Development Bank. The report is based on the findings of peer-to-peer exchanges, capacity-building activities, technical workshops and a series of study visits to OECD countries, including Canada, France, Italy, the Netherlands and Spain which have been conducted since 2014. The OECD would like to thank the officials from the Government of Egypt and the OECD peers for their support and commitment as well as the MENA Transition Fund of the G7 Deauville Partnership for the financial support.

Growing evidence demonstrates that well-designed regulations underpin inclusive growth, good governance, enabling business environment, transparency and accountability. While good regulation contributes to well-functioning markets and societies, poor regulation may undermine them by imposing undue costs on businesses and citizens.

The 2012 OECD Recommendation of the Council on Regulatory Policy and Governance (the Recommendation) is the first comprehensive international statement on regulatory policy. It stresses the link between regulatory policy and economic development; and provides guidance for countries on how to implement better regulatory governance. The Recommendation:

- provides governments with clear and timely guidance on the principles, mechanisms, actors and institutions required to improve the design, enforcement and review of their regulatory framework to the highest standards;

- advises governments on the effective use of regulation to achieve better social, environmental and economic outcomes; and

- calls for a "whole-of-government" approach to regulatory reform, with emphasis on the importance of consultation, co-ordination, communication and co-operation to address the challenges posed by the inter-connectedness of sectors and economies (OECD, 2012).

Good quality legislation is a component of sound regulatory policy. In the MENA region, good regulation is increasingly recognised as a precondition for strengthening the rule of law and building more resilient societies. Poorly drafted legislation creates legal ambiguity and insecurity; and poses challenges to cost justified, cost effective and consistent delivery of intended policy objectives. The 2009 and 2016 Regional Charter for Regulatory Quality of the MENA-OECD Governance Programme provides a set of principles and good practice for regulatory management in countries of MENA region. The Charter stresses that law drafting techniques and procedures are key to ensure the effectiveness of legislation and regulatory quality (OECD, 2016) (see Box 1.). High-quality legal drafting processes and techniques enable effective regulatory systems, support open government, reduce regulatory burdens (including duplication or conflict of regulations); and strengthen economic development and the rule of law.

---

**Box 1. The 2016 OECD-MENA Regional Charter for Regulatory Quality**

[We endeavour to]:

i. An explicit policy on regulatory quality that has the highest political support and recognition of regulatory policy as a whole of major government agenda;

ii. The implementation of open government strategies and effective stakeholder engagement tools, including online, to provide the necessary input, feedback and buy-in for the implementation of policies, laws and other regulatory instruments;

iii. Provide the appropriate Regulatory oversight of the implementation of the explicit policy on regulatory quality and make sure the good regulation should be clear, simple and practical for users through the relevant institutional arrangements that has the appropriate powers and levers;

iv. Integrated evidence based policy making using an adopted version of regulatory impact assessments relevant to the administrative culture, which also take into account impacts on gender equality and other economic and social policy dimensions, but applying the most modern techniques that enhance regulatory quality;

v. Regulatory reviews of existing stock of regulations to reduce unnecessary and burdensome regulatory burdens including administrative burdens as well as implementing an ex-post evaluation of new regulatory proposals;

vi. Regularly publish performance evaluation of the implementation of regulatory policy to inform stakeholders of progress and developments and to encourage continuous improvement among regulators;

vii. Embed good governance of regulatory agencies, when appropriate, to ensure efficient and effective regulatory delivery and user experience of regulatory policy, which is accompanied by efficient, accessible recourse and dispute resolution mechanisms;

viii. Apply administrative and judicial reviews to regulatory policy to ensure justice and fairness in the regulatory process;

ix. Give careful consideration to the appropriate risk strategies in developing policies, laws and regulatory proposals that are realistic and admit a responsible level of risk;

x. Ensure regulatory coherence across all levels of government at the national level with the appropriate capacities and adoption of regulatory tools;

---

<table>
<tr><td>xi.</td><td>Regional regulatory cooperation across the MENA region to have consistent and coherent regulatory frameworks for better integration regionally and globally;</td></tr>
<tr><td>xii.</td><td>Inclusive policies in regulatory management that involves all relevant stakeholders, especially women and young people.</td></tr>
</table>

*Note*: The Regional Charter for Regulatory Quality was submitted for approval during the 2016 Ministerial Conference of the MENA-OECD Initiative on Governance and Competitiveness on 3rd and 4th October 2016. The endorsement of the Charter means an acceptance of general principles for regulatory quality in a non-binding manner. Each country is responsible for integrating those principles in its regulatory management system.

Legislative drafting manuals contribute to coherent law drafting and help align national regulatory systems with international standards and good practice. For instance, the Palestinian Authority has prepared two legislative drafting manuals to align reliable and consonant legislative drafting techniques across legal departments in the public administration. The legislative drafting manuals of Palestinian Authority have constituted a core component of its legal reform agenda (OECD, 2013).

In light of the 2016 Regional Charter for Regulatory Quality and 2012 OECD Recommendation of the Council on Regulatory Policy and Governance, the Arab Republic of Egypt has prepared a legislative drafting manual to strengthen regulatory quality and transparency in the rule-making process. The Manual was launched in July 2018 by the Ministry of Justice and ultimately aims at supporting the rule of law and creating an enabling business environment in Egypt.

## References

OECD (2016) Regional Charter for Regulatory Quality, https://www.oecd.org/mena/governance/RegionalCharterEN.pdf\ (accessed 22 July 2019).

OECD (2013) Regulatory Reform in the Middle East and North Africa: Implementing Regulatory Policy Principles to Foster Inclusive Growth, https://doi.org/10.1787/9789264204553-en (accessed 22 July 2019).

OECD (2012) Recommendations of the Council on Regulatory Policy and Governance, https://www.oecd.org/governance/regulatory-policy/49990817.pdf (accessed 22 July 2019).

## Notes

[1] The Egyptian Legislative Drafting Manual is accessible online on the website of the Ministry of Justice: http://www.jp.gov.eg/ar/Ministry_of_Justice_Design_of_Legislative_Guide.pdf (accessed 22 July 2019).

# Chapter 1.  Implementing a better legislation policy

*This chapter serves as the basis to understand the significance of legislative drafting manuals on implementing a sound legislation and regulatory policy. It introduces the concept of legislative quality and its relevance in pursuit of good regulation and governance. Based on the evidence across the OECD and MENA countries, the chapter then examines how legislative drafting manuals can help promote legislative quality. The chapter lays out the characteristics of good legislative drafting manuals; and concludes that legislative drafting instructions have proven effective in fostering the quality of legislation; however, effective implementation is essential to fully reap their benefits.*

## Functions of legislation and importance of legislative quality

The 2012 OECD Recommendations of the Council on Regulatory Policy and Governance defines regulatory policy as "the process by which government, when identifying a policy objective, decides whether to use regulation as a policy instrument, and proceeds to draft and adopt a regulation through evidence-based decision-making" (OECD, 2012). This definition places legislation under the umbrella of a broader regulatory policy; and demonstrates the nexus between quality legislation and good regulation. Within this framework, the significance of quality legislation is twofold:

- First, legislation, as a mean whereby law is expressed, enables alignment with constitutional principles of legality, effectiveness and intelligibility; and constitutes the basis of government action (Voermans, 2009). Thus, legislative quality assists the implementation of rule of law, fosters legislation's ability to express the law and comply with the constitution.

- Second, legislation, as a regulatory instrument, serves as a mean to achieve desired regulatory results and policy outcomes (Xanthaki, 2015). Hence, legislative quality increases the capacity of legislation to deliver the intended regulatory and policy objectives.

The 2015 OECD Regulatory Policy Outlook recognises regulatory policy as one of the key levers available to governments alongside tax and spending to achieve government-wide priorities such as social welfare, environmental protection and inclusive economic growth. In governments' attempt to realise their agenda and policy goals, legislation could be used as one of the policy means available to execute government policy (Xanthaki, 2014). High quality legislation facilitates the delivery of the intended policy objectives in a cost justified, cost effective and consistent manner; and contributes to effective and efficient regulatory systems, which serve the public interest and contribute to well-functioning markets and societies.

Although the principles of clarity, precision, conciseness and coherence provide a common framework of features displayed by "good legislation", the indicators to measure the quality of legislation differ according to (i) the approach taken to define legislation and (ii) country contexts (see Box 1.1 and Box 1.2). Legislative quality is closely associated with the principles of legality, effectiveness and intelligibility when it is primarily considered as a mean through which law is expressed (Karpen and Xanthaki, 2017) In other words, "good legislation" is based on a constitutional power to legislate (principle of legality); to be enacted (principle of effectiveness); and to provide legal certainty (principle of intelligibility).

> **Box 1.1. The 2012 OECD Recommendation of the Council on Regulatory Policy and Governance**
>
> - Commit at the highest political level to an explicit whole-of-government policy for regulatory quality. The policy should have clear objectives and frameworks for implementation to ensure that, if regulation is used, the economic, social and environmental benefits justify the costs, the distributional effects are considered and the net benefits are maximised.
>
> - Adhere to principles of open government, including transparency and participation in the regulatory process to ensure that regulation serves the public interest and is informed by the legitimate needs of those interested in and affected by regulation. This includes providing meaningful opportunities (including online) for the public to contribute to the process of preparing draft regulatory proposals and to the quality of the supporting analysis. Governments should ensure that regulations are comprehensible and clear and that parties can easily understand their rights and obligations.
>
> - Establish mechanisms and institutions to actively provide oversight of regulatory policy procedures and goals, support and implement regulatory policy, and thereby foster regulatory quality.
>
> - Integrate Regulatory Impact Assessment (RIA) into the early stages of the policy process for the formulation of new regulatory proposals. Clearly identify policy goals, and evaluate if regulation is necessary and how it can be most effective and efficient in achieving those goals. Consider means other than regulation and identify the trade-offs of the different approaches analysed to identify the best approach.
>
> - Conduct systematic programme reviews of the stock of significant regulation against clearly defined policy goals, including consideration of costs and benefits, to ensure that regulations remain up to date, cost justified, cost effective and consistent, and deliver the intended policy objectives.
>
> - Regularly publish reports on the performance of regulatory policy and reform programmes and the public authorities applying the regulations. Such reports should also include information on how regulatory tools such as Regulatory Impact Assessment (RIA), public consultation practices and reviews of existing regulations are functioning in practice.
>
> - Develop a consistent policy covering the role and functions of regulatory agencies in order to provide greater confidence that regulatory decisions are made on an objective, impartial and consistent basis, without conflict of interest, bias or improper influence.
>
> - Ensure the effectiveness of systems for the review of the legality and procedural fairness of regulations and of decisions made by bodies empowered to issue regulatory sanctions. Ensure that citizens and businesses have access to these systems of review at reasonable cost and receive decisions in a timely manner.
>
> - Ensure that citizens and businesses have access to these systems of review at reasonable cost and receive decisions in a timely manner.

- As appropriate apply risk assessment, risk management, and risk communication strategies to the design and implementation of regulations to ensure that regulation is targeted and effective. Regulators should assess how regulations will be given effect and should design responsive implementation and enforcement strategies.

- Where appropriate promote regulatory coherence through co-ordination mechanisms between the supranational, the national and sub-national levels of government. Identify cross-cutting regulatory issues at all levels of government, to promote coherence between regulatory approaches and avoid duplication or conflict of regulations.

- Foster the development of regulatory management capacity and performance at sub-national levels of government.

- In developing regulatory measures, give consideration to all relevant international standards and frameworks for co-operation in the same field and, where appropriate, their likely effects on parties outside the jurisdiction.

*Source:* OECD (2012) Recommendations of the Council on Regulatory Policy and Governance, https://www.oecd.org/governance/regulatory-policy/49990817.pdf

---

**Box 1.2. Legislative quality**

**The United Kingdom**

The 'good law' initiative has been launched by the UK government in 2013. It aims to make legislation more accessible and understandable for UK citizens. The good law initiative intends everyone interested in the making and publishing of law to come together with a shared objective of making legislation work well for the users to build a shared accountability for the quality of law.

The Office of the Parliamentary Counsel (OPC) is a group of government lawyers who specialise in drafting legislation in the UK. They work closely with departments to translate policy into clear, effective and readable law; and promote 'good law'.

The Office of the Parliamentary Counsel defines the principles of good law as follows:

- necessary;

- clear;

- coherent;

- effective; and

- accessible.

In order to produce good laws, the Office of the Parliamentary Counsel is working towards fostering greater openness about how laws are drafted and debated to help avoid unnecessary confusion and litigation. The Counsel is also working with government

> policy teams about alternatives to legislation; and with the online publishers of legislation to know what drafting techniques make the user's experience better.
>
> *Source:* UK Government (2015) The Office of the Parliamentary Counsel, https://www.gov.uk/guidance/good-law
> UK Government (2018) The Office of the Parliamentary Counsel: drafting guidance, https://www.gov.uk/government/publications/drafting-bills-for-parliament

## Link between legislative and regulatory quality

The indicators to measure legislative quality closely intertwine with those of regulatory quality when legislation is primarily used in its capacity as an instrument to achieve regulatory aims (Xanthaki, 2015). This approach places legislative quality under the framework of regulatory quality and entails that legislation complies with the standards of good regulation. OECD (2015) underlines that good regulation:

- serve clearly identified policy goals, and are effective in achieving those goals;

- are clear, simple, and practical for users;

- have a sound legal and empirical basis,

- are consistent with other regulations and policies;

- produce benefits that justify costs, considering the distribution of effects across society and taking economic, environmental and social effects into account;

- are implemented in a fair, transparent and proportionate way;

- minimise costs and market distortions;

- promote innovation through market incentives and goal-based approaches; and

- are compatible as far as possible with competition, trade and investment-facilitating principles at domestic and international levels.

Under this framework, the principles of efficacy, effectiveness, clarity, precision, consistency, transparency, open government, cost-efficiency, legality and efficiency determine regulatory quality, and, hence, legislative quality. The principle of efficacy refers to the extent to which regulatory aims of legislation are met; and whether legislation delivers the intended policy goals (Xanthaki, 2014). Efficacy is essential to ensure that regulation which is cast in form of legislation achieves the government-wide objectives which it is set to address; and demonstrates the quality of legislation and regulatory environment. Effectiveness encompasses implementation, enforcement, impact, and compliance; and ensures that good legislation is capable of producing conditions necessary to achieve desired regulatory aims (Teubner, 1987). The principles of open government and transparency enable legislation to serve the public interest and to be informed by the legitimate needs of those interested in and affected by regulation (OECD, 2012). The criterion of cost-efficiency ensures that any proposed legislation achieves its objectives at minimum cost and administrative burden (OECD, 2012).

Regardless of the approach taken to measure legislative quality, good drafting techniques and procedures are essential to ensure the quality of legislation and regulation. In particular, the way legislation is drafted and the legislative drafting procedure is organised play a crucial role in creating clarity, precision, conciseness and coherence; and in fostering transparency and accountability. Good legislation requires to be cast in a manner, which most effectively achieves the intended outcomes. Poorly drafted legislation introduces loopholes into the law; undermines legal clarity, certainty and predictability; and may lead the legislation to not achieve its objectives; or to achieve them expensively (OECD, 2011a) Therefore, legislative drafting techniques and procedures are important determinants of legislative quality and may have a direct impact on the implementation of the rule of law.

The 2012 OECD Recommendation calls for a clear government policy identifying how open and balanced public consultation on the development of rules will take place. It also underlines that regulatory and legislative texts should be drafted using plain language; and should provide clear guidance on compliance with regulations to make sure that all stakeholders understand their rights and obligations. Likewise, the 2009 OECD Regional Charter for Regulatory Quality emphasises that "law-drafting procedures should be managed efficiently, to reduce delays that create uncertainty and confusion, as when implementation decrees are needed to make laws effective" (OECD, 2009).

## The role of legislative drafting manuals

Legislative drafting instructions could take different forms, varying from basic lists of drafting conventions to drafting manuals. Across the OECD, many countries have adopted legislative drafting manuals to enable transparency, effectiveness, legality and accountability in law making, comply with the principles of regulatory quality, and thus facilitate the implementation of the rule of law. Legislative drafting manuals provide uniform standards and ensure that drafting techniques and procedures are consistent, transparent and coherent across the government.

Legislative drafting manuals can contribute to legislative quality in various ways. First, legislative drafting manuals enhance the quality of legislation in its capacity as a method of harmonising drafting techniques and styles across administrative boundaries. In this regard, legislative drafting manuals provide a set of common principles and standards and foster coherence, consistency and collaboration across different public institutions and bodies. A legislative drafting manual that provides clear drafting instructions also contributes to legislation's ability to express law in a uniform, homogenous, clear, precise and predictable manner. Under this framework, manuals enable uniform quality in legislation, which is essential to uphold constitutional principles and ensure that citizens and businesses can identify their rights and obligations and the courts can enforce them. Therefore, legislative drafting manuals can help implement legal norms and strengthen the rule of law, accountability and transparency.

Second, legislative drafting manuals can serve as an instrument to place good legislation under the umbrella of regulatory governance and to link legislation to the intended policy objectives. In this capacity, legislative drafting manuals acknowledge that legislation may act as a legal expression of regulatory choices, which aims to produce desired regulatory and policy outcomes. Thus, legislative drafting manuals forge a conceptual link between legislation, regulation and policy, and enable legal drafters across all levels of public administration to take desired policy objectives of legislation into account throughout the legislative drafting process. This allows legal drafters to grasp the potential policy impact of proposed legislation. Legislative drafting manuals also provide a common framework on the way legislation across administrative boundaries should be composed to achieve their objectives in most effective and efficient manner. Under this framework, legislative drafting manuals foster the principles of efficacy and effectiveness through ensuring that regulation cast in the form of legislation delivers the intended policy goals.

Third, legislative drafting manuals can serve as a framework on which the scrutiny of legislation can be based (see Box 1.3). Scrutiny of legislation assesses whether a particular piece of legislation is effective for accomplishing the ends for which it is or will be created. Legislative scrutiny helps prevent duplication or conflict of legislation and can be considered as an exercise of legislative quality control. Legislative drafting manuals, as a mean for legislative scrutiny, provide guidance on how to examine whether new provisions proposed by new legislation are consistent with the existing legal system; and contribute to obtain better outcomes from legislation.

---

**Box 1.3. Germany**

Germany has adopted *the Manual for Drafting Legislation* as a set of guiding principles for legislative drafting. The first edition of the guide was published in 1999 and it has been revised twice since then. The current version of the Manual has been released in 2008 as the third edition.

The Manual has been designed to provide a uniform framework of standards, which the federal ministries can apply when drafting legislation and on which the scrutiny of legislation can also be based in order to examine whether new provisions are consistent with the current legal system. The Manual also aims to ensure that legal provisions are well structured and worded so that their meaning is clear and easy to understand; and that it is available to reach citizens, businesses and legal practitioners.

German Manual for Drafting Legislation contains various checklist questions and good practice examples; and provides a comprehensive guideline for all those involved in the drafting and scrutiny of legislation across federal ministries. Drafting instructions are based on legal requirements as well as on practical legislative experience based on the feedback deriving from the use of the Manual everyday legislative work.

German Manual also creates a link between good legislation and regulation by underlining that it aims to contribute to creating legally consistent and comprehensible regulations.

*Source:* The Federal Ministry of Justice, Germany (2008) The Manual for Drafting Legislation, https://www.bmjv.de/SharedDocs/Downloads/DE/Themen/RechtsdurchsetzungUndBuerokratieabbau/Han dbuchDerRechtsfoermlichkeit_eng.pdf?__blob=publicationFile&v=4

---

## Good practices

Evidence across the OECD and MENA countries demonstrates that the content and purpose of legislative drafting manuals may vary across different jurisdictions (see Box 1.4, Box 1.5, Box 1.6 and Box 1.7). As this could be due to the different approaches taken by the authors of the manuals, one of main differences also derives from the fact that legislative drafting process is organised in a different manner in common law and civil law systems. In civil law countries, policy formulation and legislative drafting are closely linked. The same officials who develop the policy are also involved in the drafting of the necessary legislation. Once the legislation is drafted, it is then reviewed by officials in other Ministries such as those in Justice who are generally concerned with ensuring that the legislation achieves its purpose in a constitutional manner.

In common law system, policy-making and legislative drafting are separated. Once a political decision is made to enact legislation, officials in the Executive Branch of

Government prepare a policy paper setting out the problem, alternative solutions, and the final decision as to which policy will be adopted. The policy paper is then sent to legislative drafting specialists who compose the legal text (Karpen and Xanthaki, 2017). Due to these differences, legislative drafting manuals in specific jurisdictions are likely to differ in terms of content and purpose as they are tailored to the context of their legislative systems. Hence, the criteria to define "a good legislative drafting manual" depend on the jurisdiction in question to a large extent.

---

### Box 1.4. The Palestinian Authority

The Palestinian Authority has adopted a legislative drafting manual in 2013 to promote coherent and consistent legislative techniques across legal departments.

This manual is based on previous manuals of the Palestinian Authority (PA). The first manual, which is mainly concerned with drafting of primary legislation, was published in 2000. The second manual focusing on the policy development and drafting of secondary legislation was published in 2004. These manuals reflect the co-operative work undertaken by the Government of the Palestinian Authority, the Palestinian Legislative Council and the Palestinian academic community.

In 2010, the OECD conducted an assessment of the legislative drafting manuals of the Palestinian Authority and provided advisory and technical support for a consolidated and improved manual. In light of the *OECD Practitioners' Guide* on public consultation in the rule making, the Palestinian Authority has created a committee for public consultation, coordinated by the President's Office and chaired by the Ministry of Justice and has drafted their own guide on public consultation.

The guide was reviewed and quality checked by OECD peers from Norway, UK, Sweden and Turkey during 2011-2013. The Guide has been tested and used by the General Personnel Council (GPC) during the preparation of a consultation plan on the draft Code of Conduct. The results of this pilot project were reported to the committee and fed in the final PA Guide on public consultation.

A separate committee was established for the legislative drafting manual and chaired by the Council of Minister. This committee has met with the committee for the consultation guide on a regular basis to prepare a new manual, which follows the principles of the PA Guide on public consultation. A new legislative drafting manual was developed with a participatory approach involving the engagement of diverse stakeholders. The new manual was endorsed in 2013 by the Cabinet. A series of capacity building activities for both internal and external stakeholders was organised by the OECD to operationalise the new legislative drafting manual and the consultation guide of the Palestinian Authority.

The 2013 manual focuses on the preparation of drafting instructions; the structure and elements of a law; the principles of drafting style; the drafting of specific provisions such as amendments and penal provisions; and reviews of the completed draft. They also include advice on the preparation of notes submitted with the draft law as well as a methodology to evaluate the impact of draft legislation.

*Source:* OECD (2011) Legislative Drafting Manuals of the Palestinian Authority, https://www.oecd.org/mena/governance/50402734.pdf
OECD (2011) Regulatory Consultation in the Palestinian Authority: A Practitioners' Guide for Engaging Stakeholders in Democratic Deliberation

---

**Box 1.5. Switzerland**

In 2019, Switzerland has adopted the fourth edition of its legislative drafting guide, *Guide de legislation*. The Swiss Manual defines legislative acts as the expression and legal fulfilment of political decisions; and aspires to provide practical guidelines to legislative drafters.

The Swiss Manual targets all parties involved in the drafting of legislative acts within the federal administration; and aims to guide the development of the federal legislation. In particular, the Manual intents to serve as collective memory of legislative practice in the federal administration to facilitate the transmission of acquired experience.

The structure of the Manual is based on a division of the legislative process into various stages: analysis of problems, definition of objectives, examination and choice of instruments of action, analysis of the normative environment, structuring and formulation; and execution.

It focuses on following aspects:

- Fundamental Rights and International Law

- Sharing of powers between the confederation and the cantons

- Choice of the form of the legislative act

- Legality and delegation

- Composition of the legislative act and choice of the instruments of the actions of the State

- Writing

Ultimately, the Swiss Manual aims to contribute to improve the quality of legislation, which in turn allows for better enforcement and more accurate translation of the will of the legislator.

*Source:* The Federal Office of Justice, Switzerland (2019) *Legislative guide*
https://www.bj.admin.ch/dam/data/bj/staat/legistik/hauptinstrumente/gleitf-d.pdf

**Box 1.6. The Netherlands**

The Dutch government has introduced a number of policies and tools to improve the overall legislative quality. One of the key measures was the adoption of a general legislative policy, which consists of a set of measures; and aims at creating lasting improvements to legislative system by setting legislative quality criteria.

In 1992, the Netherlands adopted "Instructions for Legislation" *(Draaiboek voor de wetgeving)* which set the basis of legislative drafting instructions applicable for legal departments across the public administration. "Instructions for Legislation" is a comprehensive handbook on legislative techniques, styles and substantive legislative issues. It comprises an extensive set of drafting guidelines accompanied by several examples, explanations, illustrations, model clauses. Instructions are amended regularly and available electronically.

In addition, the Netherlands has also adopted "Drafting Directives" *(Aanwijzingen voor de Regelgeving)* which was issued by the Ministry of Justice. These Directives provide a detailed description of all procedures for the Council of Ministers, the Council of State and the Parliament leading to the approval of a Bill.

The Dutch government has established the Dutch Academy of Legislation to provide a comprehensive training programme for all state officials in charge of legislative drafting to ensure effective application of Instructions and Directives.

*Source:* Dutch Government (2017) Aanwijzingen voor de Regelgeving; https://www.kcwj.nl/kennisbank/aanwijzingen-voor-de-regelgeving-0 Dutch Government (2017) Draaiboek voor de wetgeving; http://wetten.overheid.nl/BWBR0005730/2011-05-11 Wim Voermans (2009) Different Approaches to Legislative Drafting in the EU Member States, http://www.sigmaweb.org/publicationsdocuments/44577810.pdf

**Box 1.7. The European Union**

The European Union has developed *"The Joint Practical Guide"* as a platform of general drafting principles. The first edition of the Guide was published in 2000; and has proven to be a valuable tool. It has been updated once since then and the second edition was published in 2013. The Guide is publicly available in 24 official languages of the EU.

The Joint Practical Guide is intended for everyone involved in legislative drafting across the EU. It creates the basis of common standards for the EU in the field of legislative drafting as well as for the legislative drafting workshops, trainings and courses provided to EU officials. The principles set out in the guide are the point of reference on legislative drafting for the three EU institutions: the European Parliament, the Council and the Commission.

The Guide aims to ensure that the Acts of the European Union are drawn up in an intelligible and consistent manner so that citizens and businesses can identify their rights and obligations and the courts can enforce them. Ultimately, the legislative drafting guide of the EU aspires to assure that the EU legislation is better understood and correctly implemented.

The content of Joint Practical Guide of the EU is very generalised and standardised due to the diversity of the jurisdictions in its member states. In this respect, the EU Manual offers a unique example as it takes account of diverse legislative systems including common law and civil law countries; and provides a common framework on the uniform legislative drafting standards.

The Joint Practical Guide suggests that the drafting of a legal act must be:

- clear, easy to understand and unambiguous;

- simple and concise, avoiding unnecessary elements;

- precise, leaving no uncertainty in the mind of the reader.

Following the adoption of the legislative drafting guide of the European Union, the *"Joint Practical Guide of the European Parliament, the Council and the Commission"*, an interinstitutional group on the quality of drafting was set up to be responsible for keeping the guide updated. The Guide urges the legal drafters of the European Parliament, the Council and the Commission to use the guide and to contribute to it with their comments by sending them to the interinstitutional group on the quality of drafting.

*Source:* European Union (2013) "Joint Practical Guide of the European Parliament, the Council and the Commission" https://eur-lex.europa.eu/content/techleg/EN-legislative-drafting-guide.pdf

## Characteristics of good legislative drafting manuals

Despite the lack of uniform criteria applicable to all jurisdictions to define "a good legislative drafting manual", there are some guiding principles, which could enhance the effectiveness of legislative drafting manuals. First, legislative drafting manuals, which are fine-tuned to the regulatory framework of specific jurisdiction, best serve to the needs and context of the jurisdiction in question and help legislation deliver the intended policy goals. This entails that legislative drafting manuals should be based on a sound analysis of:

- the target audience of the manual and what answers they are looking for;

- the specific purpose of the manual; and

- the level of legal background and awareness of the legal terminology the target audience of the manual has.

In other words, legislative drafting manuals, which are most effective to contribute to legislative and regulatory quality, build on an empirical analysis of target audience and their needs; and are tailored to the regulatory framework of specific jurisdictions. For instance, in common law systems, drafting specialists primarily compose legislation. In this case, a good legislative drafting manual could still be technical as the target audience of the manual has advanced level of expertise in legal drafting and terminology. In civil law systems, however, experts in the certain policy field primarily draft legislation. Therefore, a good legislative drafting manual in civil law countries is expected to be neither too long nor technical but rather short, simple and precise while providing explanations and introducing main principles of drafting step-by-step.

The legislative drafting manual of the UK provides a good example as it was prepared on the basis of an empirical analysis which assessed effectiveness and clarity of legislative techniques through an online survey and face-to-face user testing (see Box 1.8). The study compared various techniques and styles of drafting and analysed the feedback deriving from all respondents to the survey who are actively engaged with legislation. The findings of the survey and the study have paved the way for an updated legislative drafting guidance, which is tailored to particular needs of the UK legislative system and regulatory framework.

---

**Box 1.8. The United Kingdom**

The Office of the Parliamentary Counsel (OPC) is the central drafting office composing most of the United Kingdom's primary legislation and some secondary legislation. The Office of the Parliamentary Counsel and the National Archives carried out a study in 2014 to: (i) understand more about what it is like to be a reader of legislation; and (ii) to assess whether some drafting techniques are more helpful for readers than others.

The rationale behind the assessment derives from the desire and necessity to establish objective standards for better legislation. For instance, the experience of the Office of the Parliamentary Counsel demonstrates that principle of clarity is based on the drafter's own judgement. Furthermore, the principle of effectiveness cannot be ensured without knowing who is using the legislation and for which purpose. Hence, the study was designed to find empirical answers to these questions and to establish objective standards on effective legislative drafting techniques.

The study was conducted by an *online survey* on legislation.gov.uk comparing small scale drafting techniques and by *face-to-face user testing* designed to compare other drafting techniques. The participants involved diverse parties who actively use legislation including members of parliament, ministers, policy officials, bill managers, parliamentary officials, lobby groups, judges, government lawyers and private lawyers.

The findings of the study have demonstrated the difficulties readers of legislation face and led to improvements on the way in which UK legislation is presented online, as well as significant changes to the UK's legislative drafting guidance.

The key findings point out that:

---

- Users want to understand 'why' the legislation has been passed rather than just 'what' it does to the law.

- Users want explanatory notes to be more practical, to contain examples about how the law is to be applied in the real world.

- Users want more legal context about the intent or purpose of the legislation.

- Users use the explanatory notes to Acts on an ongoing basis, not only when the Act is first passed.

- Users want practical information that explains any amendments to existing legislation, or new regulations that may be passed as a result.

On the basis of these results, a new Legislative Drafting Guidance has been introduced in 2017. In order to reflect the changing needs of legal drafters, the Guidance has been updated on July 2018. The Guidance stresses that guiding principles are tailored to particular needs of the UK legislative system and regulatory framework and contains guidance on how to draft bills, including:

- guidance on writing clearly;

- specific wording to use in certain circumstances;

- drafting techniques;

- guidelines on drafting repeals and amendments; and

- information about subordinate legislation.

*Source:* UK Government (2018) The Office of the Parliamentary Counsel, https://www.gov.uk/government/publications/drafting-bills-for-parliament
UK Government (2014) The Office of the Parliamentary Counsel and the National Archives, "What works best for the reader? A study on drafting and presenting legislation: the Loophole" https://assets.publishing.service.gov.uk/government/uploads/system/uploads/attachment_data/file/326937/Loophole_-_2014-2__2014-05-09_-What_works_best_for_the_reader.pdf

Second, the OECD experience demonstrates that good legislative drafting manuals are developed with a participatory approach involving consultations with different entities and stakeholders across the government and seen as living documents, which are updated on a regular basis. This enables manuals to adapt to the changes in the legal and regulatory environment as well as to the changing needs of legislative drafters (see Box 1.6 and 1.9).

Third, good legislative drafting manuals present their strategy and purpose upfront; and introduce guiding principles in a clearly delineated manner so that legislative drafters know what to prioritise; and when to make exceptions (Xanthaki, 2015) (see Box 1.9). Prioritisation of principles should be outlined in a way that enhances the effectiveness of legislation and fosters legislative quality. This reflects the dynamic nature of law making, enables legislative drafting manuals to serve as guiding principles, and prevents them from becoming too rigid. In this respect, it is crucial to ensure that legislative drafting manuals assist legal drafters by providing guidance, practical advice and examples throughout the legislative drafting and policy processes. In other words, good legislative drafting manuals should act as a catalyst to the work of legal drafters and should not be burdensome.

**Box 1.9. France**

The French legislative guide presents set of rules, principles, methods and modalities to accompany regulators and public officials through all stages of preparing legal norms (i.e. conception, elaboration and drafting). The guide helps answer procedural, formal, and substantive questions for drafters to consider when drafting a text, starting from the conception of the norm, to its elaboration, and drafting. It also specifies the procedures that need to be followed for the elaboration and transposition of European and international texts into national legislation. In particular, the guide focuses on following aspects:

1. **Conception:** In the conception phase, the legislative guide walks the legislator through the process to answer certain preliminary questions such as the necessity of the proposed norm, whether it responds to a legal obligation, or is a mean to achieve certain policy goals, and what would be the appropriate type of norm to serve its purpose.

   The conception phase is essential to assess the objectives and justifications of the proposed legislation as it analyses and evaluates the usefulness and effectiveness of the normative text. This phase also allows to compare norm alternative solutions, thus, prevents the accumulation of unnecessary legislations and legal uncertainty.

   It is worthwhile to stress that one of the distinctive features of the French legislative guide derives from its practicality. In particular, *Le Guide de Légistique* provides step-by-step guidance on each administrative process. For instance, the guide specifies with whom, when and under which circumstances to organise stakeholder consultations as well as which formal procedures to follow, what to discuss, and desired outcomes. Furthermore, the guide lays out a framework for the form and content of the impact assessments and stipulates each step of specific procedures to be followed.

2. **Elaboration:** In this phase, the legislative guide specifies the roles of different institutions concerned with the process, according to the type of norm in question. The guide also sets specific instructions tailored for each type of legal norm guiding the legal drafters from the phase of prior consultation to the publication of the final text.

3. **Drafting:** The guide sets a framework for drafting the legal texts by specifying the rules on the preparation of explanatory memorandums to the parliament (explaining the meaning and scope of the provisions), the language that is advised to be used (styles, vocabulary, and syntax), and how to introduce modifications, insertions, annexes, and references to the existing laws at later stages.

Overall, the detailed and practical nature of the French legislative guide provides a uniform framework as well as a solid coordination structure for legislative procedures, which, in turn, enables a sustainable and coherent approach to regulatory policy.

It is also important to underline that the French legislative guide is designed to be a living document in order to adapt to new developments including fast technological advancement, as well as to the changing needs of its users. The French legislative guide has so far undergone several updates since the publication of its first edition in 2005. The second edition of the guide was published in 2007 and the third and most current edition was released in 2017.

In addition, the electronic version of the legislative guide is constantly updated to take account of latest legislative, regulatory and jurisprudential reforms. It is also important to stress that France has established a formal process for updating the legislative guide. There is an institutionalised joint team, comprised of the participants from the Council of State and of the General Secretariat of the Government (SGG), dedicated to updating the guide.

In order to facilitate an effective application of the guide, the General Secretariat of the Government regularly organise trainings targeted to central and local authorities. These trainings help legislators and policy makers understand how to best apply the guide in their day-to-day legislative practice. Furthermore, the methodology and modules of trainings are constantly revised to adapt to the needs of legal drafters and changing regulatory policy environment.

Furthermore, *Le Guide de Légistique* is part of a broader ecosystem of better regulation and legislation policy. It is supported by the application of Regulatory Impact Analysis (RIA) as well as transparent open-government policies in order for citizens and businesses to identify their rights and obligations easily.

The French legislative guide is available online as part of an institutionalised one-stop-shop government website which allows for rapid and effective dissemination of legislative and regulatory texts, as well as court rulings, collective labour agreements, standards issued by European institutions, international treaties and agreements to which France is a party.

Source: Government of France (2018), Guide de Légistique - Édition 2017 https://www.legifrance.gouv.fr/Droit-francais/Guide-de-legistique2; and information provided during a meeting with the General Secretariat of the Government (SGG) in September 2018

It is also worthwhile to underline that legal drafters need to be informed on how to best use legislative drafting manuals in their daily work. This requires a coherent approach and operational strategy across legal departments in public administration providing legal drafters with an understanding of the significance and purpose of the application of the manual on enhancing effectiveness and quality of legislation and regulation (see Chapter 2. ).

## References

European Union (2013) "Joint Practical Guide of the European Parliament, the Council and the Commission" https://eur-lex.europa.eu/content/techleg/EN-legislative-drafting-guide.pdf (accessed 22 July 2019).

Federal Ministry of Justice, Germany (2008) The Manual for Drafting Legislation, https://www.bmjv.de/SharedDocs/Downloads/DE/Themen/RechtsdurchsetzungUndBuerokratieabbau /HandbuchDerRechtsfoermlichkeit_eng.pdf?__blob=publicationFile&v=4 (accessed 22 July 2019).

Federal Office of Justice, Switzerland (2019) Legislative guide
https://www.bj.admin.ch/dam/data/bj/staat/legistik/hauptinstrumente/gleitf-d.pdf (accessed 22 July 2019).

Government of France (2018), Guide de Légistique - Édition 2017  https://www.legifrance.gouv.fr/Droit-francais/Guide-de-legistique2 (accessed 22 July 2019).

Government of the Netherlands (2017) Aanwijzingen voor de Regelgeving;
https://www.kcwj.nl/kennisbank/aanwijzingen-voor-de-regelgeving-0 (accessed 22 July 2019).

Government of the Netherlands (2017) Draaiboek voor de wetgeving;
http://wetten.overheid.nl/BWBR0005730/2011-05-11 (accessed 22 July 2019).

Government of the UK (2018) The Office of the Parliamentary Counsel,
https://www.gov.uk/government/publications/drafting-bills-for-parliament (accessed 22 July 2019).

Government of the UK (2018) The Office of the Parliamentary Counsel: drafting guidance,
https://www.gov.uk/government/publications/drafting-bills-for-parliament (accessed 22 July 2019).

Government of the UK (2015) The Office of the Parliamentary Counsel,
https://www.gov.uk/guidance/good-law (accessed 22 July 2019).

Government of the UK (2014) The Office of the Parliamentary Counsel and the National Archives,
"What works best for the reader? A study on drafting and presenting legislation: the Loophole"
https://assets.publishing.service.gov.uk/government/uploads/system/uploads/attachment_data/file/326937/Loophole_-_2014-2__2014-05-09_-What_works_best_for_the_reader.pdf (accessed 22 July 2019).

Karpen, U. and H. Xanthaki (2017) Legislation in Europe: A Comprehensive Guide for Scholars and Practitioners

OECD (2015), OECD Regulatory Policy Outlook 2015, OECD Publishing, Paris.
http://dx.doi.org/10.1787/9789264238770-en

OECD (2012) Recommendations of the Council on Regulatory Policy and Governance,
https://www.oecd.org/governance/regulatory-policy/49990817.pdf

OECD (2011a) Legislative Drafting Manuals of the Palestinian Authority,
https://www.oecd.org/mena/governance/50402734.pdf

OECD (2011b) Regulatory Consultation in the Palestinian Authority: A Practitioners' Guide for Engaging Stakeholders in Democratic Deliberation

OECD (2009) Regional Charter for Regulatory Quality,
https://www.oecd.org/mena/governance/45187832.pdf

Teubner, G. (1987) Regulatory law: Chronicle of a Death Foretold' in Lenoble (ed), Einfuhrung in der Rectssoziologie (Darmstadt, Wissenschaftliche Buchgesellschaft,) 54.

Voermans, W. (2009) Different Approaches to Legislative Drafting in the EU Member States,
http://www.sigmaweb.org/publicationsdocuments/44577810.pdf (accessed 22 July 2019).

Xanthaki, H. (2015) "Drafting Manuals and Quality in Legislation: Positive Contribution towards Certainty in the Law or Impediment to the Necessity for Dynamism of Rules?" Legisprudence, 4:2, 111-128, DOI: 10.1080/17521467.2010.11424705

Xanthaki, H. (2014) Drafting Legislation: Art and Technology of Rules for Regulation

# Chapter 2.  The Egyptian Manual for Legislative Drafting

*This chapter focuses on legislative drafting in Egypt. It first maps out the process of legislative drafting in Egypt while demonstrating how legislative drafting processes and procedures work. It then identifies the existing challenges in the current legislative and regulatory framework; and demonstrates how the Egyptian Legislative Drafting Manual could help overcome these challenges; and thus contribute to better legislation and regulation.*

## Legislative Drafting Process in Egypt

Legislation is classified into two categories: primary legislation and secondary legislation. Primary legislation includes the Constitution, laws, legislative decrees, and treaties and agreements[1]. According to the Egyptian Constitution, laws can be initiated by the parliament[2], the Cabinet or the President[3]. Secondary legislation is issued by the Executive, and can be further categorised into three types:

- Executive legislation: These include detailed rules necessary to implement laws which tend to provide the general rules concerning the issue under regulation to ensure flexibility. Executive regulations are issued by the prime minister unless the law specifies who shall issue the regulation (Egyptian Constitution, Article 170, 2014). As they are issued by the Executive Authority, these regulations can be amended or repealed easily compared to laws which are issued by the parliament.

- Organisational legislation: These can only be issued by the prime minister, after approval of the cabinet, to organise public utilities and authorities (such as establishing authorities or agencies, specifying their mandate and functions, or abolishing them) (Egyptian Constitution, Article 171, 2014). Unlike executive regulations, these regulations are not issued based on an ordinary legislation.

- Control legislation: These are the rules laid down by the prime minister, after approval of the cabinet, to protect order and public health (such as regulations concerning food safety) (Egyptian Constitution, Article 172, 2014). They do not implement a specific law.

Both the parliament and the executive (i.e. the president or cabinet) can propose legislation. Legislation initiated by the former, the parliament, is called "proposal law" if it is proposed by less than ten percent of the members of parliament. Legislation proposed by the Cabinet, the President of Republic and more than ten percent of the members of parliament are called "project law".

The Constitution also gives the President of the Republic the right to issue legislation, called "legislative decree", in extraordinary circumstances. For instance, in cases where there is a need to take quick action that cannot be delayed when the parliament is not in session, legislative decrees might be issued. Laws issued by the President need to be submitted to the parliament for review and approval within 15 days. If not, legislative decrees have no retroactive impact, unless the parliament approves their validity in the previous period or the settlement of their impacts.

The enactment of ordinary legislation in Egypt consists of the following steps:

1. Initiation and drafting of proposal,
2. Review by the Parliament,
3. Issue by the President, and
4. Publishing and enforcement.

### *Initiation and Drafting of Legislation*

Legislation can be initiated both by parliament and the government. The process of initiating and drafting legislation by the government and parliament is explained in the following two sub-sections.

### *Legislation proposed by the government*

Although there are no existing standard procedures or guidelines for the development of legislation in ministries; there are common practices which guide the process.

In most cases, a ministry initiates the process for introducing new legislation or amending existing one due to one of the following reasons:

- to realise minister's vision which could be based upon recommendation of their advisers or heads of subordinate authorities and agencies;

- in response to the public interest or problems with the existing legislation;

- in the implementation of recommendations by international development organisations;

- to reflect the verdicts of the Supreme Court;

- in response to the reports of regulators concerning problems in regulation; and

- to be in line with the country's international commitments.

The process of the development of legislation involves a consultation process between ministries. The concerned minister may form a working group, including technical officials from the ministry with expertise in the field as well as legal experts led by the legal adviser to the minister, who are mainly concerned with composing the legal text.

This consultation process might sometimes be supported by consultants, who prepare studies about the expected outcomes and benefits of the legislation and associated risks. Throughout the development of legislation, the working group reviews existing legislation and examines it article by article identifying challenges and proposing amendments. This mainly aims at addressing the limitations of the existing legislation. However, consultation is not mandatory and at the discretion of the entity. Therefore, given that there is no guiding framework, consultations can take different forms and be ad hoc.

The cabinet or ministers may send draft laws and proposals to the Legislation Department at the Ministry of Justice to benefit from their expertise on drafting legislation and legal issues. The Department reviews the quality of drafts in terms of internal consistency, clarity and intelligibility; and may redraft the proposal, if necessary. The Legislation Department also checks the constitutionality of draft legislation.

Once the legal text is drafted, the legal adviser presents the results of the working group to the minister. Upon the approval by the minister, legislative proposal is sent to the Cabinet, together with an explanatory memorandum, for review and discussion by ministers. Although there is no required standard format for the explanatory note, it usually explains the rationale behind the development of new legislation (i.e. the current challenges necessitating introducing change), and the objectives of the proposed sections or articles.

Before placing it on the agenda of the Cabinet, the proposed legislation needs to be presented to the Prime Minister. Upon the approval of the Prime Minister, the proposed legislation is included on the agenda of the Cabinet and a session is reserved to discuss the proposal and the concerned minister is notified. The draft is discussed in the Cabinet and can be approved; returned to the ministry for amendment; or rejected. The Secretariat for Legislative Affairs may ask the proposing ministry for clarifications concerning the drafting of the legislation. In most cases, the draft goes through several iterations. Once it reaches a satisfactory stage and approved by the Cabinet, draft legislation is forwarded to the State Council for legal review. The draft is then returned to the Cabinet, which in turn sends it back to the concerned ministry to incorporate the Council's comments, and forwards it back to the Cabinet. The final version of the draft is approved by the Cabinet and sent along with the explanatory note to the House of Representatives for ratification.

### *Legislation proposed by the members of the parliament*

The legislation initiated by members of the parliament, is called "proposal law" if it is proposed by less than ten percent of the members of parliament. Legislation proposed by the Cabinet, President of Republic and more than ten percent of the members of parliament (MPs) are called "project law".

The proposal submitted by more than ten percent of MPs needs to be drafted in articles and accompanied by an explanatory memorandum, including the constitution's text related to the proposal, and the main principles on which it is based and the desired objectives (Law No. 1/2016, Article 181). If a law is proposed by less than ten percent of MPs, then it needs to follow special procedures (Law No. 1/2016, Article 158).

### *Review by Parliament*

Project laws, proposed by the government, and proposal laws, proposed by the members of the parliament, are presented in the House of Representatives meeting where the Speaker refers them to the relevant specialised committee in the parliament for review. The Speaker may also circulate the draft and its explanatory memorandum to all MPs (Law No. 1/2016, Article 158).

Specialised committees review the proposal laws and project laws referred to them in their areas of competence in the order they were received (Law No. 1/2016, Article 186). Reviews of assessing the objectives and impact of the proposed legislation might take place in the committees but could benefit from a common framework to ensure even and systematic application of impact assessments.

The specialised committee might request the government to provide additional information to which the government has to respond within 15 days following the receipt of the request (Law No. 1/2016, Article 78). Committees may also invite government officials, heads of departments or authorities to attend their meetings during the discussion of relevant topics. They can also bring along experts and specialists on the subject from their ministries or agencies[4]. Although the government officials could be consulted during the discussions, they have no voting power on the adoption of the proposed legislation (Law No. 1/2016, Article 61). The Speaker may also ask other committees to provide an opinion about a report submitted by another committee in the assembly's discussion (Law No. 1/2016, Article 55-56). In addition, the Speaker can form ad hoc committees comprising a number of MPs from specialised committees to examine a bill or a certain issue (Law No. 1/2016, Article 80). The Speaker may also form joint committees, comprising two or more specialised committees to examine draft legislation (Law No. 1/2016, Article 81).

Upon the approval of the Speaker of the House, the specialised committee may refer the draft to the Constitutional and Legislative Affairs Committee for review (Law No. 1/2016, Article 162). The Constitutional and Legislative Affairs committee submits a report to the Speaker of the House including its findings and recommendations. The Speaker may refer the report to the General Committee[5] to receive its opinion (Law No. 1/2016, Article 47). Once the report is finalised, the Speaker decides whether to include it on the assembly's agenda. If included on the agenda, the report has to be distributed to MPs at least 24 hours before the specified meeting (Law No. 1/2016, Article 70). The assembly may decide to return the report to the committee for further study in light of the discussions (Law No. 1/2016, Article 71).

The proposed legislation is discussed in the assembly meeting, as a whole and then article by article. MPs may suggest amendment, addition or deletion of articles by submitting the suggested amendments to the Speaker at least 24 hours before the meeting[6]. The proposed amendments are then discussed in the assembly (Law No. 1/2016, Article 159). The concerned specialised committee shall be notified with the proposed amendments before the meeting so that it can examine them, and the coordinator of the committee presents the opinion of the committee on the suggested amendments during the discussion (Law No. 1/2016, Article 160). If the assembly decides to refer the proposed amendment to the committee, the committee has to submit its report on whether the amendment has an impact on the other articles of legislation. In this case, discussion of the draft shall be postponed until the committee finishes its review. Otherwise, the assembly continues the discussion of the other articles of the draft legislation (Law No. 1/2016, Article 161).

Deliberation starts with discussion of the principles and general bases of the draft legislation as a whole. If the assembly rejects the proposal in principle, the draft is considered to be rejected (Law No. 1/2016, Article 166). On the other hand, if approved, the draft legislation is discussed article by article and MPs have to vote on each article and then on the draft as a whole (Law No. 1/2016, Article 167). If approved by the absolute majority of present MPs, which should not be less than a third of the total number of MPs, the proposal is considered approved by the House. If votes are equal, the proposal is considered rejected (Egyptian Constitution, Article 122, 2014). Some laws (such as those regulating judicial bodies or elections) require votes of no less than two-thirds of MPs for approval. All laws are submitted to the State Council for review.

### Issue by the President

After approval of the proposal law or project law by the House of Representatives, it is sent to the President of the Republic who has the right to issue it or reject it. If the President approves the law it is published, otherwise it is referred back to the parliament within 30 days. In case of rejection, the President informs the Speaker on the reasons of objection. Despite objection of the President, the House of Representatives may organise another vote and might pass the law if it is approved by no less than two thirds of the whole House (Egyptian Constitution, Article 123, 2014). If, however, the House accepts the objection of the President, the Speaker forms a committee to re-examine the proposal and amend it.

### Publishing

The legislation is required to be published in the official gazette within 15 days from its issue by the President (Egyptian Constitution, Article 225, 2014). Laws and presidential decrees are published in the "Official Gazette" while secondary legislation (including ministerial and governor decrees and decisions of public authorities and agencies) are published in "Waqa'a Al-Masreya", which is an annex to the Official Gazette. Constitution stipulates that legislation enters into force 30 days from the day following their issue, unless another date is specified in the legislation. It is mandatory to publish primary legislation in the official gazette. Access to official gazette is subject to subscription fee.

## Current Challenges

The current legislative drafting process poses several challenges to the quality of legislation and regulation in Egypt. First, the absence of a common framework on legislative drafting leads to the application of inconsistent methodologies for the preparation of legislation across the government, as observed in other OECD and MENA countries. For instance, legislation might be composed by a technical working group or a legal adviser working with policy-making officials. The absence of guiding principles for the development of legislation affects the coherence in the regulatory framework.

Second, the experience across the OECD demonstrates that the absence of written legislative standards poses challenges to the scrutiny of legislation and legislative quality. The differences in criteria for legislative drafting may lead to uneven application of quality assurance and undermine uniform quality. Furthermore, the quality of legislation risks becoming dependent on the expertise and skill of the legal counsellor composing the text rather than on the common standards. Based on OECD experience, legislative and regulatory framework could benefit from a common framework on which the scrutiny of legislation can be based.

Third, review of legislation needs to be conducted based on a regulatory reform policy rather than on an ad hoc basis. As observed in other OECD and MENA countries, the absence of a systematic review of the stock of legislation results in an accumulation of outdated legislation[7] and demonstrates that the development of legislation does not adequately assess the necessity of the adoption of new legislation or considers alternatives. The challenges to the systemic review of the stock of legislation are closely associated with the challenges deriving from lack of registry of all legislation in force. The absence of comprehensive registry of all regulations in force may lead legal counsellors to resort to the practice of implicit repeal in drafting (article is included at the end of the regulation stating that any provisions contradicting the provisions are hereby repealed). This poses challenges to legal certainty, as legal drafters composing legislation may not be fully aware of all provisions in force, whether they are amended or implicitly repealed. Systemic review of existing legislation benefits citizens and businesses by accurately identifying their rights and obligations.

Fourth, based on OECD experience, the lack of formal consultation with stakeholders jeopardises the quality of legislation. Consultation is not mandatory and takes places on an ad hoc basis through informal consultation at various stages of the drafting process depending on the topic and the significance and scale of the impact of legislation. Evidence across the OECD demonstrates that legislative quality can be fostered through institutionalised consultation mechanisms.

Fifth, regulatory policy can be improved through a common framework on impact assessment to identify how various groups in the society will be affected as a result of the proposed legislation and to minimise its negative unintended consequences. Egyptian Regulatory Reform and Development Activity (ERRADA) introduced regulatory impact assessment (RIA) and conducted impact assessment studies on several topics such as the allocation of arable land; shipping agencies; and increasing heights of buildings. Further standard guidelines can support the uniform application of impact assessment across the government.

## Egyptian Legislative Drafting Manual

The Legislative Drafting Manual prepared by the Ministry of Justice of Egypt can help overcome the existing challenges in the current legislative and regulatory framework and contribute to better legislation in a number of ways. First, the Egyptian Legislative Drafting Manual[8] specifies the target audience of the Manual and introduces its strategy and purpose upfront. The Manual is intended for stakeholders involved in the preparation, drafting, and review of bills across all branches and levels of the government. It provides drafting instructions and aims at introducing a common framework of principles on legal drafting to ensure uniform quality in law making. In particular, the Manual aspires to act as a practical tool accompanying legal drafters throughout the process by providing guidance, explanations, practical advice and examples of what to do and what to avoid. This is a crucial step to overcome the current challenges deriving from the lack of consistent legislative drafting methodologies and uneven legislative drafting expertise across the government.

Second, the Legislative Drafting Manual of Egypt is tailored to the regulatory framework and country-specific priorities of Egypt while drawing on good practices in the field. The Manual stresses the link between policy and legislation and defines legislation as a mean to achieve specific policy objectives. Moreover, the Manual introduces guidelines on how to write the "Statement of Objectives and Justifications" of proposed legislation to effectively communicate the policy objectives of legislation in a clear and transparent manner.

Third, the Egyptian Legislative Drafting Manual establishes a set of guiding principles to assess the need to draft new legislation and to consider alternatives to legislation. In order to assess the necessity of the adoption of new legislation, it suggests that necessary studies and research must be carried out to demonstrate that it is not efficient to address the concerned problem through other means such as amendments or the use of non-legislative alternatives. The Manual also underlines the need to keep the stock of legislation up-to-date. In this respect, the Manual aims to reduce administrative burden and cost; and help overcome challenges stemming from the duplication or conflict of law, and accumulation of outdated legislation. Fourth, the Egyptian Legislative Drafting Manual introduces a common framework on the preparation of the Explanatory Memorandum, which is submitted to the House of Representatives by the Cabinet along with the proposed legislation for review. There is no required standard format for the content of Explanatory Memorandum in the current legislative framework. The Manual aims to formulate uniform standards for the format and content of Explanatory Memorandums.

Furthermore, the Manual establishes principles on the practice of repeal in legislative drafting. For instance, the Manual discourages the use of the phrase "any provision contradicting the provisions of this law is to be repealed". Instead, it suggests legal drafters to identify all laws related to the new bill, examine the relationship between the proposed legislation and all other applicable laws and determine whether the applicable provisions contradicts the provisions of the proposed bill. This aims to contribute to legal certainty and enable legal drafters, citizens and businesses to be aware of all provisions in force.Finally, the Legislative Drafting Manual of Egypt aims to address the challenges deriving from the lack of formal consultation mechanisms through providing guidelines on how to organise consultations with relevant stakeholders throughout the process. The Manual underlines the significance of targeting all concerned parties; and stresses the need to expand the scope of consultations to enforcement entities, experts, non-governmental organisations, unions, syndicates as well as judges specialised in the relevant field.

## References

Law No. 1/2016 concerning issue of the internal regulation of the House of Representatives, Article (181).

Law No. 1/2016 concerning issue of the internal regulation of the House of Representatives, Article (158).

Law No. 1/2016 concerning issue of the internal regulation of the House of Representatives, Article (158).

Law No. 1/2016 concerning issue of the internal regulation of the House of Representatives, Article (186).

Law No. 1/2016 concerning issue of the internal regulation of the House of Representatives, Article (78).

Law No. 1/2016 concerning issue of the internal regulation of the House of Representatives, Article (61).

Law No. 1/2016 concerning issue of the internal regulation of the House of Representatives, Articles (55-56).

Law No. 1/2016 concerning issue of the internal regulation of the House of Representatives, Article (80).

Law No. 1/2016 concerning issue of the internal regulation of the House of Representatives, Article (81).

Law No. 1/2016 concerning issue of the internal regulation of the House of Representatives, Article (162).

Law No. 1/2016 concerning issue of the internal regulation of the House of Representatives, Article (47).

Law No. 1/2016 concerning issue of the internal regulation of the House of Representatives, Article (70).

Law No. 1/2016 concerning issue of the internal regulation of the House of Representatives, Article (71).

Law No. 1/2016 concerning issue of the internal regulation of the House of Representatives, Article (159).

Law No. 1/2016 concerning issue of the internal regulation of the House of Representatives, Article (160).

Law No. 1/2016 concerning issue of the internal regulation of the House of Representatives, Article (161).

Law No. 1/2016 concerning issue of the internal regulation of the House of Representatives, Article (166).

Law No. 1/2016 concerning issue of the internal regulation of the House of Representatives, Article (167).

The Egyptian Constitution, 2014, Article (122).

The Egyptian Constitution, 2014, Article (123).

The Egyptian Constitution, 2014, Article (170).

The Egyptian Constitution, 2014, Article (171).

The Egyptian Constitution, 2014, Article (172).

The Egyptian Constitution, 2014, Article (225).

# Notes

[1] Laws and legislative decrees have the same power. The main difference between them is that whereas the former is issued by the parliament the latter is issued by the President of the Republic.

[2] According to the current constitution enacted in 2014, Egypt has a semi-presidential political system. The President of the Republic is the head of the Executive Authority; he is elected in a direct popular vote, every four years, and can be re-elected for one term only (The Egyptian Constitution, Articles (139-140)). The House of Representatives is unicameral and sits for a term of five years. Members of parliament (MPs) are elected by absolute majority of legitimate vote casts. The President can appoint up to 5% of the total number of MPs in parliament (which is currently 596) and can also dissolve it if necessary and after a popular referendum (The Egyptian Constitution, 2014, Article (137)).

[3] The Prime Minister and Cabinet are appointed by the President, after the approval of the House of Representatives (parliament) (The Egyptian Constitution, Article (146)); and they are accountable to the legislature (The Egyptian Constitution, Articles (129-131)).

[4] Sometimes, ministries ask the Ministry of Justice to represent them before the specialized committees.

[5] The General Committee comprises the Speaker, two deputies and the heads of specialised committees. Its responsibilities include reviewing reports submitted by the specialised committees on monitoring of implementation of laws and regulatory decrees. Law No. 1/2016 concerning issue of the internal regulation of the House of Representatives, Article (26).

[6] The Speaker may decide to look into suggested amendments raised just before or during the meeting after listening to the explanation of those proposing the amendment Law No. 1/2016 concerning issue of the internal regulation of the House of Representatives, Article (163).

[7] Some of the economic activities listed in schedules in Law No. 453/1954 concerning industrial and commercial premises are outdated.

[8] The report considers the Manual in an English translation. However competent the translation, there is always the possibility that some nuances could be lost. It should therefore be recognised that some aspects of the assessment might be based on such information.

# Chapter 3.  The Way Forward

*This chapter outlines how to best implement the Egyptian Manual for Legislative Drafting in an effective and efficient manner, based on the experiences of OECD countries. The chapter underlines that it is essential for Egypt to build their ongoing legislative reform efforts on a comprehensive and whole of a government regulatory policy strategy in order to complement the significant progress achieved with the preparation of the Legislative Drafting Manual. The chapter concludes with specific recommendations to help maximise the potential of the Egyptian Manual for Legislative Drafting as a tool for obtaining better outcomes from legislation.*

## Implementation of the Egyptian Legislative Drafting Manual

The Egyptian Legislative Drafting Manual is among the first of its kind in the MENA region. Despite the progress, evidence across other countries demonstrates that the presence of legislative drafting manuals alone cannot improve the quality of legislation. Achieving the objectives of legislative drafting manuals and obtaining better outcomes from legislation demand a clear and coherent approach that is supported by a sound implementation strategy. A strategy can equip legal drafters with an understanding of how to best use legislative drafting manuals in their daily work, structure key priorities and guide the implementation of legislative drafting manuals.

In addition to effective implementation, high-level political commitment is equally important to ensure that legislative drafting manuals can deliver their intended goals. Experience across the OECD countries shows that the success of the guidelines depends on the extent to which all parties engaged in legislative drafting commit themselves to follow them. In this respect, a formal announcement and commitment by the government, which calls for proper application of the legislative drafting instructions could raise awareness, prevent them from going unnoticed, and thus increase their impact.

Furthermore, the experience of the OECD countries illuminates that implementing a good legislation policy is a gradual process necessitating the presence and systemic application of a set of regulatory policy tools in place rather than the delivery of a single product. Legislative drafting manuals are one of the significant tools that could contribute to improve the quality and effectiveness legislative and regulatory system. However, it is worthwhile to note that a good legislation and regulation policy requires a-whole-of-government approach integrating a set of regulatory policy tools systemically and as a whole across the government, namely: Regulatory Impact Analysis (RIA) ex post and ex ante, review of stock of legislation, administrative simplification, transparency and communication, alternatives to regulation, and compliance and enforcement (OECD, 2012). Therefore, it is essential for Egypt to build their ongoing legislative reform efforts on a comprehensive and whole of a government regulatory policy strategy in order to complement the significant progress achieved with the preparation of the Legislative Drafting Manual.

In light of the findings of this report, the following recommendations are applicable to implement the Egyptian Legislative Drafting Manual in most effective and efficient manner.

## Specific Recommendations

- **Ensure that the Manual is embedded into a broader "whole-of-government" policy for regulatory governance and supported by application of regulatory policy tools such as public consultation mechanisms and impact assessments.** As outlined by the 2012 OECD Recommendations of the Council on Regulatory Policy and Governance, implementing a good legislation policy is a gradual process necessitating the presence and systemic application of a set of regulatory policy tools in place rather than the delivery of a single product. Regulatory Impact Analysis (RIA) ex post and ex ante, review of stock of legislation, administrative simplification, transparency and communication, alternatives to regulation, and compliance and enforcement require to be applied as a whole across the government.

- **Ensure high-level political commitment and sustained support for the effective implementation of the Manual. This should also assure that all parties engaged in legislative drafting commit to follow them.** Based on OECD experience, a formal announcement and commitment by the government, which calls for proper application of the legislative drafting instructions is critical to ensure legislative drafting manuals can deliver their intended goals.

- **Design and publish a coherent approach and a "whole of a government" operational strategy on the implementation of the Egyptian Legislative Drafting Manual.** The strategy should cover the key steps to be taken on the implementation of the Manual while allocating clear responsibilities across relevant stakeholders and introducing timelines. It is important that the strategy provides legal drafters with an understanding of the significance of the application of the Manual on improving the quality of legislation. It should also include a communication strategy to raise awareness and to ensure sustained support for the successful implementation of the Manual.

Support could be generated at three levels:

- At the highest political level to ensure strong commitment to the implementation of the Manual;

- Across the legal departments in public administration to incentivise legal drafters to implement the legislative drafting guidelines; avoid resistance to the change; and ensure that they feel the ownership of the Manual; and

- Across the society to generate trust in the legislative reform agenda.

The strategy should introduce short and medium term goals to facilitate the monitoring of the progress.

- **Commit to report regularly on the implementation of the measures outlined in the operational strategy and the Legislative Drafting Manual.** Regular monitoring and evaluation of the implementation allows for measuring the effectiveness of implementation through tracking progress over time; reveals potential bottlenecks and encourages the formulation of appropriate responses.

- **Update and revise the Manual regularly based on the constant feedback provided by its users on their experience of working with this tool on a daily basis.** Experience of the OECD countries demonstrate that legislative drafting manuals which best contribute to legislative and regulatory quality are living documents which are able to adapt to the dynamic nature of legal drafting and daily needs of legislative drafters.

- **Establish solid consultation and feedback mechanisms as well as an institutionalised working party tasked with keeping the Manual updated.** Many OECD countries have introduced specific consultation and feedback mechanisms to help obtain constant feedback from the users of their manuals. Establishing a working party involving relevant stakeholders ensures the transparency of the process and enables collaboration across different institutions. The working party and methods used for consultation process needs to be institutionalised for effective feedback as well as monitoring and evaluation mechanisms. In addition, a network could be formed to help create buy-in to the Manual across different institutions and departments, and to keep the Manual up-to-date.

For instance, following the adoption of the legislative drafting guide of the European Union, the *"Joint Practical Guide of the European Parliament, the Council and the Commission"*, an inter-institutional group on the quality of drafting was set up to be responsible for keeping the guide updated (European Union, 2013). The inter-institutional group involves representatives of three European Union institutions so as to ensure that the drafting specialists of the three institutions work together to agree upon a common approach to all drafting matters.

- **Pilot the Manual across different institutions and ministries; and report the feedback of users to the working party to update and revise the Manual.** The Egyptian Legislative Drafting Manual is a new tool and first of its kind in Egypt. Expecting immediate systemic application of the Manual across the government could be unrealistic given the uneven capacities and skills across public institutions. Piloting the Manual in different ministries and bodies could be a useful initial approach to introduce the Manual, test its applicability; and reveal potential challenges to address them accordingly.

- **Ensure that the Manual is publicly accessible and widely disseminated.** It is of vital importance that all parties engaged in legislation have access to the Manual and could benefit from it. This should ensure that the Manual is publicly available online as well as on the internal webpages of public institutions. Easy access to the Manual is crucial to raise awareness about the presence and significance of the Manual and ensure its effective utilisation.

- **Create an institutionalised one-stop-shop government website for sharing and disseminating legal and regulatory information as well as the Manual.** A one-stop-shop official website with free online public access, providing a database on all legislations and regulations, judicial verdicts and decisions could help disseminate legal information across the government institutions as well as the society (see Box 3.1). This website could also provide a platform for disseminating the Manual.

For instance, in France, *"La Documentation Française"* serves a legal and administrative database providing a comprehensive information on all regulations and case laws. Furthermore, an official electronic journal is accessible through "legifrance.gouv.fr" which allows for a rapid and effective dissemination of legislative and regulatory texts, as well as court rulings, collective labour agreements, international treaties and agreements to which France is a party. The website also provides access to the French legislative guide.

---

**Box 3.1 Publishing and Disseminating Legal Information**

In 2017, the Legal and Social Research Unit of the American University in Cairo has launched its digital platform Manshūrāt Qānūneya (MQ) with the objective of providing a free online access to a host of otherwise unavailable primary legal materials. The MQ has five core functions, namely archive, timeline, legal news, legal organigram, and legal commentaries. The platform aims to raise awareness and to assist in legal research and litigation, which could contribute to greater legal reform efforts in the long term. MQ provides access to a vast collection of primary legal materials (around 30,000 documents) and covers a wide spectrum of subjects (47 research themes). The legal materials covered by the MQ includes constitutional, legal and regulatory documents, as well as administrative decisions, decrees, court verdicts, advisory opinions and draft laws.

MQ serves as a free, user-friendly, online legal platform, which could be easily used by both legal and non-legal practitioners. Therefore, it aims to equip citizens with a better understanding of legal and regulatory framework and contribute to strengthening citizen engagement.

As an official initiative, the Court of Cassation also offers a legal portal, containing a vast database of Egyptian legislations based on the information from the official gazette, parliamentary meeting minutes, jurisprudence of the Supreme Constitutional Court, and jurisprudence of all chambers of the Court of Cassation. However, the portal does not provide exhaustive information on the jurisprudence of other courts.

The portal of the Court of Cassation also offers a newsletter, a trilingual legal dictionary, and translations of the French and American jurisprudence. The portal is freely and publicly accessible, and helps disseminate legal and regulatory information across the government and citizens.

*Source:* Manshūrāt Qānūneya, https://manshurat.org/; Court of Cassation, http://www.cc.gov.eg/Legislations/Egypt_Legislations.aspx

- **Introduce special software packages incorporating drafting guidance into the computer systems.** Drafting assistance tools have been introduced across a number of OECD countries to apply legislative drafting manuals more effectively and easily. These software packages also provide legal drafters with practical help and correspond to their daily needs.

  For example, the European Union institutions use specialised software packages offering access to the relevant parts of the legislative drafting guide of the European Union and to other drafting guidance, such as standard formulas or templates called the Drafting Assistance Package (DAP). It also offers drafters the possibility to consult the drafting specialists by email or telephone with a guarantee of a rapid response. Drafting support tool of a similar kind could greatly benefit the application of the Egyptian Legislative Drafting Manual as well.

- **Provide trainings, seminars and workshops on legislative drafting principles, the use of the Manual and legislative drafting software tools to all stakeholders engaged in legislative drafting.** It is essential to ensure that legislative drafters have adequate capacities and skills to be able to accurately apply the Manual and to produce quality legislation. Institutionalised legislative drafting training programmes at the government, civil service training bodies or universities introducing legal drafters to the use of Manuals and legislative drafting software tools can contribute to awareness raising and the advancement of necessary skills among the legal drafters.

This could also help ensure that all those concerned with the preparation of legislation are made aware of the importance of good legislation.

Awareness could be generated at three levels:

- Across the public officials who will have to apply the rules;

- Across businesses which will have to comply with the rules; and

- Across the society who may be affected by the rules.

In applying these recommendations, Egypt might consider establishing a set of priorities and codifying them into a strategic and actionable implementation plan identifying a timeline with short and medium-term action-oriented goals. However, many actions suggested by the above-mentioned recommendations are complementary to each other and would have to be pursued simultaneously.

## References


European Union (2013) "Joint Practical Guide of the European Parliament, the Council and the Commission" https://eur-lex.europa.eu/content/techleg/EN-legislative-drafting-guide.pdf (accessed 22 July 2019).

Court of Cassation (2019), http://www.cc.gov.eg/Legislations/Egypt_Legislations.aspx (accessed 22 July 2019).

OECD (2012) Recommendations of the Council on Regulatory Policy and Governance, https://www.oecd.org/governance/regulatory-policy/49990817.pdf (accessed 22 July 2019).

Manshūrāt Qānūneya (2019), https://manshurat.org/ (accessed 22 July 2019).

# ORGANISATION FOR ECONOMIC CO-OPERATION AND DEVELOPMENT

The OECD is a unique forum where governments work together to address the economic, social and environmental challenges of globalisation. The OECD is also at the forefront of efforts to understand and to help governments respond to new developments and concerns, such as corporate governance, the information economy and the challenges of an ageing population. The Organisation provides a setting where governments can compare policy experiences, seek answers to common problems, identify good practice and work to co-ordinate domestic and international policies.

The OECD member countries are: Australia, Austria, Belgium, Canada, Chile, the Czech Republic, Denmark, Estonia, Finland, France, Germany, Greece, Hungary, Iceland, Ireland, Israel, Italy, Japan, Korea, Latvia, Lithuania, Luxembourg, Mexico, the Netherlands, New Zealand, Norway, Poland, Portugal, the Slovak Republic, Slovenia, Spain, Sweden, Switzerland, Turkey, the United Kingdom and the United States. The European Union takes part in the work of the OECD.

OECD Publishing disseminates widely the results of the Organisation's statistics gathering and research on economic, social and environmental issues, as well as the conventions, guidelines and standards agreed by its members.

OECD PUBLISHING, 2, rue André-Pascal, 75775 PARIS CEDEX 16
(42 2019 01 1 P) ISBN 978-92-64-31143-5 – 2019

Printed by Libri Plureos GmbH in Hamburg,
Germany